I'm the Chef!

This edition first published in the UK in 2002 by
Franklin Watts
96 Leonard Street
London EC2A 4XD

ISBN 0 7496 4652 7

Project Manager: Anne McRae
Graphic Design: Marco Nardi
Photography: Marco Lanza, Walter Mericchi
Set Design: Rosalba Gioffrè
Editing: Holly Willis, Anne McRae
Layout and cutouts: Adriano Nardi, Laura Ottina

Special thanks to: Mastrociliegia (Fiesole) and Dino Bartolini (Florence)
who kindly lent props for photography.

A CIP catalogue record for this book is available from the British Library.

Colour separations: Fotolito Toscana (Florence)
Printed and bound by Artegrafica, Verona

I'm the Chef!

A YOUNG CHEF'S
FRENCH
COOKBOOK

Rosalba Gioffrè

W

FRANKLIN WATTS
LONDON•SYDNEY

List of Contents

DISCLAIMER

The recipes in this book are suitable for children aged nine and above. They have been prepared in our test kitchen by a mother of three young children and are safe for children of that age. Since cooking involves the use of knives, boiling water and other potentially dangerous equipment and procedures, we strongly recommend that adults supervise children at all times while they prepare the recipes in this book. The publishers and copyright owners will not accept any responsibility for accidents that may occur as children prepare these dishes.

Introduction

French food is so good that it has become famous all over the world. Despite its reputation as a complicated **cuisine**, there are many dishes that young chefs can prepare successfully. In this book, there are 15 classic recipes with step-by-step photographs. Follow the instructions carefully and you will be able to serve delicious meals for your friends and family. Each recipe has special tips and tricks to help you get it right from the start. The central pages (pp. 22–23) focus on The Feast of the Kings, a festival that children in France celebrate on January 6. So, tuck in, or as the French say, *Bon appétit!*

Croque-Monsieur
Toasted cheese and ham sandwich

This toasted sandwich was invented in a bar on the Boulevard des Capucines in Paris in 1910. Not only is it tasty, it is also very easy to make. It's a sort of French fast food, and you can experiment with different variations. For example, try topping it with a fried egg: this is called a 'croque-Madame'!

1 Leave the butter to soften at room temperature. It should be soft but not melted. Use a knife to spread it onto one side of the bread.

2 If you are not using sliced cheese, grate the cheese. Make sure you keep your fingertips well away from the grater.

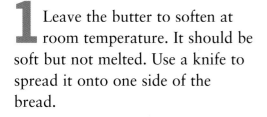

 TIPS & TRICKS

Ask an adult to help you when putting the croque-Monsieur into, or taking it out of, the oven. If you do it yourself, wear thick oven gloves to protect your hands.

8

Ingredients

15 g (½ oz) butter

2 slices bread

30 g (1 oz) Gruyère or Swiss cheese

2 slices of ham

3 Cover one of the slices of bread with the ham. **Trim** off any extra ham and place it in the middle. **Sprinkle** the grated cheese or lay the sliced cheese over the ham.

Place most of the cheese in the centre of the sandwich to stop it from oozing out.

Utensils

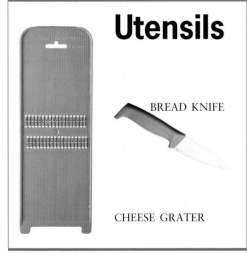

BREAD KNIFE

CHEESE GRATER

4 Place the other slice of bread on top, with the buttered side facing inwards. Cook the croque-Monsieur in a preheated oven at 350°F (180°C/gas 4) for about 15 minutes, turning it over half way through.

Crêpe au fromage

Cheese crêpes or pancakes

Crêpes are one of the most famous of all French dishes, so to be a real French chef you must learn how to make them. Luckily, they are not very difficult. Crêpes can be served with salty fillings, such as cheese and ham, or with sweet ones, such as sugar, jam, chocolate and whipped cream. Even today, there are crêpe stalls on many street corners in Paris and other cities in France.

TIPS & TRICKS

*Each time you add batter to the frying pan, add a little more melted butter first. Hold the pan firmly by the handle as you cook the crêpes. If you do not have **Gruyère cheese**, use a thin slice of cheddar cheese, or any other cheese that melts well, instead.*

Ingredients

125 g (4 oz) plain flour

pinch of salt

250 ml (9 fl oz) milk

2 eggs

30 g (1 oz) butter

8 thin slices Gruyère or other cheese

8 thin slices ham

Utensils

FRYING PAN

MIXING BOWL

WHISK

WHISK

SLOTTED SPATULA

6 Return the folded crêpes to the pan long enough to melt the cheese. Serve them warm.

2 Still stirring, add the eggs, followed by the melted butter, and stir until the batter is smooth. Place in the fridge for one hour.

1 **Sift** the flour and salt into a bowl. Pour in the milk a little at a time, stirring continuously with a whisk or fork.

3 Melt a little extra butter in a 22-cm (9-in) frying pan and add a **ladleful** of batter.

4 Move the frying pan around so a thin layer of batter covers the bottom. Cook until light brown on one side. Use a spatula to flip and cook the other side. Place the crêpe on a plate. Repeat until the batter is finished.

5 Cover half of each crêpe with a slice of cheese and a slice of ham. Fold the empty half over the top.

Place the crêpes on a pre-heated serving dish. Serve for lunch with a green salad.

Gratin de macaroni

Macaroni cheese

Béchamel is a well-known French white sauce. It was invented by Louis de Béchamel, who was head **butler** at the grand court of King Louis XIV in the 17th century. Béchamel goes particularly well with pasta, but is also delicious with vegetables baked in the oven.

1 Melt the butter in a saucepan over a low heat. Remove from the heat and sift in the flour, stirring continuously so that no lumps form.

2 Return to the heat and cook for 1–2 minutes, so that the flour is lightly browned.

3 Pour in the milk a little at a time, stirring continuously. Add salt, pepper and nutmeg to taste. After a few minutes, the mixture will boil. Cook for 3-4 minutes, stirring all the time.

Utensils

CHEESE GRATER

WOODEN SPOON

COLANDER

OVENPROOF BAKING DISH

SAUCEPAN

4 Lightly butter an ovenproof dish and cover the bottom with a layer of cooked macaroni. If you are using long macaroni, curl the strands around to cover the dish as evenly as you can. You can also use other types of pasta, short or long.

5 Cover the macaroni with a layer of sauce, followed by a layer of Gruyère and a sprinkling of Parmesan. Repeat until all the ingredients are used up.

Ingredients

125 g (4 oz) butter

105 g (3½ oz) plain flour

salt and black pepper

pinch of freshly grated nutmeg

500 ml (18 fl oz) milk

300 g (10 oz) cooked macaroni

150 g (5 oz) Gruyère cheese

60 g (2 oz) grated Parmesan cheese

TIPS & TRICKS

To cook the macaroni, place a large pan of cold water over a high heat. When it is boiling, add the macaroni and cook for the time indicated on the packet. When the macaroni is cooked, ask an adult to help you drain it in the colander.

6 Preheat the oven to 400°F (200°C/gas 6) and bake for about 20 minutes, or until a golden crust, or 'gratin' has formed. Ask an adult to remove the hot dish and serve straight from the oven.

Omelette aux tomates

Tomato omelette

Omelettes are quick and easy to make. They are also **nutritious** and fun to serve. They can be eaten plain, with herbs, or filled with cheese, tomatoes, ham or any of your favourite ingredients. Omelettes are also practical when unexpected friends drop by. If eggs are the only food you have in your fridge, you can offer them this delicious treat.

1 On a chopping board, slice the onion thinly with a sharp knife. Hold the knife firmly by the handle, and keep your fingers well away from the blade. Ask an adult to help.

TIPS & TRICKS

While cooking the omelette, make sure that the handle of the frying pan does not stick out. You might knock it onto yourself, or the floor, as you pass by.

Ingredients

1 onion

4 ripe tomatoes

2 tablespoons olive oil

salt and ground black pepper

6 eggs

1 bunch parsley

2 Place a pan of water over a high heat. When the water boils, turn off the heat and carefully add the tomatoes. Leave for 2 minutes, then remove with a slotted spoon. When the tomatoes have cooled down, remove the skins with your fingers. **Chop** the tomatoes into tiny pieces.

3 Heat the oil in a frying pan. Add the onion and tomato, season with salt and pepper, and cook over a medium to low heat for 15 minutes. Hold the handle of the pan while you stir it with a wooden spoon.

4 Break the eggs into a bowl and beat them quickly with a fork. Season with a little salt.

Utensils

CHOPPING BOARD

KNIFE

FRYING PAN

WOODEN SPOON

5 Lightly oil another frying pan and place over a medium to low heat. Pour in half the eggs and cook for 4–5 minutes. Move the pan gently from side to side as the omelette cooks. Remove the omelette from the heat and slide it onto a serving dish.

6 Cook the second omelette as shown above. Pour half the tomato sauce onto one half of each omelette, sprinkle with chopped parsley and use a wooden spoon to fold it in two. Serve and enjoy!

Quiche Lorraine

Bacon quiche

The word quiche comes from the German word *Kuchen*, which means **savoury** tart or flan. There are many different types of quiche, but quiche Lorraine is the classic one. It was invented by a French cook in the northern city of Nancy in the 16th century. The French serve quiche as a **first course**, but it is so filling and nourishing that it can be served as a meal in itself.

1 Sift the flour and salt into a mixing bowl. Add the chopped butter and rub it in using your fingers until the mixture is the **consistency** of bread crumbs. Gradually add just enough water to bring the mixture into a ball and leave in the fridge for 30 minutes.

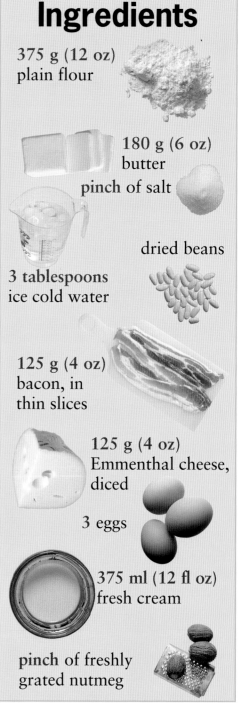

Ingredients

375 g (12 oz) plain flour

180 g (6 oz) butter

pinch of salt

3 tablespoons ice cold water

dried beans

125 g (4 oz) bacon, in thin slices

125 g (4 oz) Emmenthal cheese, diced

3 eggs

375 ml (12 fl oz) fresh cream

pinch of freshly grated nutmeg

TIPS & TRICKS

This quiche is also good if made with ham instead of bacon. Ask an adult to help when putting dishes in, or taking them out, of the oven and remember to use oven gloves.

2 Lightly flour a rolling pin and roll the pastry out on a floured work surface until it is about 5 mm (¼ in) thick.

3 Use the pastry to line a buttered, floured 26-cm (10-in) diameter loose-bottomed flan dish.

4 Prick the pastry on the bottom of the dish with a fork. Cover with a sheet of baking paper and fill with the dried beans. Bake in a preheated oven at 400°F (200°C/gas 6) for 20 minutes.

5 Take the pastry out of the oven and throw away the paper and beans. Fry the bacon lightly (you could cut it up into small pieces) and add to the flan, with the cheese.

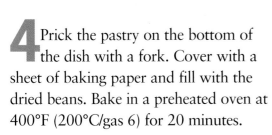

6 Beat the eggs and cream. Add a pinch of salt and nutmeg. Pour the mixture over the bacon and cheese. Bake in a preheated oven at 350°F (180°C/gas 4) for 30 minutes.

Utensils

ROLLING PIN

KITCHEN SCALES

LOOSE-BOTTOMED FLAN DISH

BAKING SHEET

Salade niçoise

Tuna, egg and tomato salad

This healthy, colourful salad is easy to prepare and requires almost no cooking. Served with freshly baked French bread, it makes a nutritious lunch or snack. Its name comes from Nice, a beautiful city on the Mediterranean Sea in the south of France. Many fish dishes are unique to this region. The ingredients can be changed so that if you do not like onions, for example, you can replace them with another herb or vegetable.

1 Wash the vegetables and dry them thoroughly. Slice the red pepper across the middle and remove the seeds and core. Slice it into thin, round strips.

2 Peel and slice the cucumber into thin pieces. Cut the tomatoes into **wedges** and the onion into thin wheels. Place the lettuce leaves in a salad bowl.

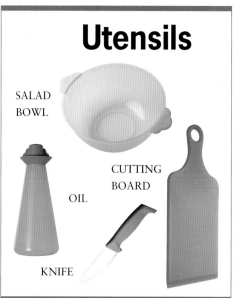

Utensils

SALAD BOWL

OIL

CUTTING BOARD

KNIFE

4 Sprinkle with a little salt and drizzle with the oil. Use salad servers to toss the ingredients. Try to do this carefully so that the eggs do not fall apart.

3 Peel the eggs and cut them in quarters lengthwise. Place the eggs and the other ingredients on top of the lettuce leaves.

TIPS & TRICKS

Be very careful with the knife when you are chopping the vegetables. Ask an adult to help. Hold the knife firmly by the handle and use your other hand to hold the vegetables. Always watch what you are doing, and make sure that your fingertips stay well away from the blade of the knife.

Ingredients

10 fresh large lettuce leaves

1 red pepper

1 cucumber

1 red onion

2 ripe salad tomatoes

2 hard-boiled eggs

200 g (7 oz) tuna, preserved in olive oil

12 black olives

salt

3 tablespoons olive oil

Poulet en brochettes

Chicken kebabs

Brochettes, or kebabs, are a common dish from southern France and the Mediterranean island of Corsica. Kebabs are fun to make because you can alternate the meat and other ingredients on the skewers to make each one look different. When cooked, you can slide the ingredients off the skewer with a fork. The grapefruit in this recipe can be replaced with cherry tomatoes or another vegetable.

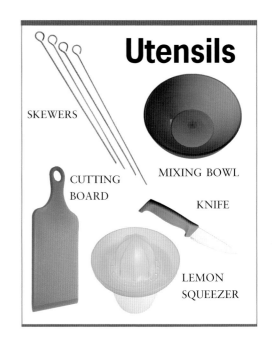

Utensils

SKEWERS

CUTTING BOARD

MIXING BOWL

KNIFE

LEMON SQUEEZER

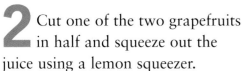

1 Place the chicken breasts and pancetta or bacon on a chopping board. Chop them into bite-sized pieces.

2 Cut one of the two grapefruits in half and squeeze out the juice using a lemon squeezer.

3 Beat the grapefruit juice with the olive oil and a little salt and pepper in a bowl. Add the chopped meat and mix well. Set aside to **marinade** for at least 30 minutes. If you have the time, two hours is even better.

4 Peel the remaining grapefruit, removing as much of the pith as possible. Ask an adult to help you use a pointed knife to remove the skin covering each wedge.

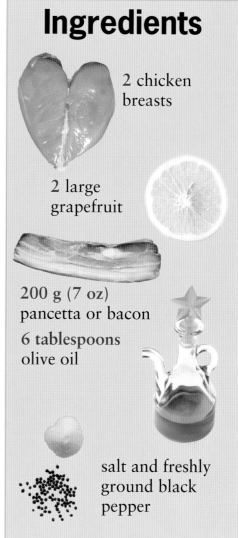
TIPS & TRICKS

If using wooden skewers, soak them well in cold water first so they do not burn. These kebabs can also be cooked over a barbecue or in the oven.

5 Stick a piece of chicken onto a skewer, then follow with a piece of pancetta, and then a piece of grapefruit. Repeat until the skewer is full. When all the kebabs are ready, place them under the grill for about 15 minutes. Turn them often during cooking and sprinkle with a little salt. Ask an adult to help you.

La Fête des Rois

La Fête des Rois, the Feast of the Kings, takes place in France at Epiphany, celebrated on 6th January. Epiphany is an ancient festival in memory of the three kings (the three wise men) who went to Bethlehem to worship Jesus soon after he was born. In France, a special *galette*, or cake, is baked with a *fève*, or bean hidden inside. Whoever finds the bean in their piece of cake is king for a day. Invite your friends to a party. Bake the *galette* and put a secret mark on top where the bean is located that only you will recognize. Since you are the host, do not take that piece. The youngest guest hides under the table and calls the name of the next person to receive a slice of cake.

Remember to put the marker or bean in the cake mixture.

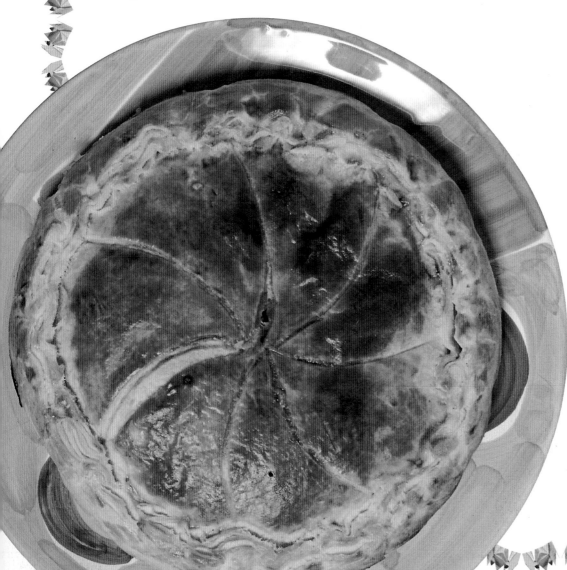

La galette des Rois

- 125 g (4 oz) butter
- 125 g (4 oz) sugar
- 3 eggs
- 125 g (4 oz) finely ground almonds
- 2 rounds puff pastry, 30-cm (12-in) in diameter

Beat the butter and sugar until creamy. Stir in two eggs, then add the almonds. Line a greased loose-bottomed dish with one of the pastry rounds. Fill with the almond mixture. Beat the remaining egg and brush it over the edges of the pastry. Place the other pastry round on top and seal well. Use a knife to make patterns in the pastry. Brush the rest of the beaten egg over the top. Bake in a preheated oven at 400°F (200°C/gas 6) for 30 minutes. Serve warm.

This beautiful painting was painted by the Italian artist, Gentile da Fabriano, in 1423. It shows the three kings worshipping the baby Jesus. The kings travelled from the East to Bethlehem. They followed a bright guiding star.

Buy some coloured paper and prepare simple crowns for your guests to wear. Make one extra special crown for the person who finds the bean in their cake.

Hachis Parmentier

Minced meat and potato pie

The combination of minced meat and potato purée tastes so good that this may become one of your favourite French dishes. Potatoes were not always as popular in France. When Monsieur Parmentier (after whom the dish was named) began growing potatoes in about 1785, no one liked them. Parmentier had to use tricks just to get people to taste them!

Ingredients

1 kg (2.2 lb) potatoes

500 ml (18 fl oz) milk

90 g (3 oz) butter

300 g (10 oz) cooked meat, or uncooked mince

1 large onion

bunch of parsley

salt

pinch of freshly grated nutmeg

1 Peel the potatoes and cook them in boiling water for about 20 minutes, or until a fork slides in easily. Drain off the water and place in a bowl.

5 Grease the ovenproof dish with a little butter and cover with a layer of potato. Sprinkle with the parsley, then add the meat. Cover with the remaining potato and top with the butter.

6 Bake in a preheated oven at 400°F (200°C/gas 6) for 20 minutes.

2 Mash the potatoes with a potato masher. Add half the butter and keep mashing. Gradually add the milk to make a smooth, creamy mixture. Season with salt and nutmeg.

TIPS & TRICKS

Remember to turn the oven on about 15 minutes before you finish preparing the pie so that it will be hot when you are ready to cook. Always ask an adult for help when using the oven.

3 If you are using cooked meat, chop or mince the meat (in a food processor) until it is in small pieces. Chop the onion and cut the parsley into fine bits.

4 Melt half the remaining butter in a pan and fry the onion and parsley. Add the meat and season with salt. Cook for 5 minutes over a medium heat, or 15 minutes if you are using raw mince.

Utensils

POTATO PEELER

HALF-MOON CHOPPER

MASHER

WHISK

MIXING SPOON

FRYING PAN

OVENPROOF BAKING DISH

Sole meunière

Butter, lemon and parsley sole

Sole is so tasty that the ancient Romans called the fish *solea jovis*, or Jupiter's sandal, in honour of one of their gods. Chefs have found many different ways of serving it in French cuisine. This recipe is called *sole meunière*, or miller's sole. The fish is dipped in flour and **sautéed** in butter to make a tasty sauce.

Sprinkle the fish with parsley before serving. Serve hot!

TIPS & TRICKS

Turning the fish in the pan is quite difficult. Ask an adult to help you with this step. Make sure you remove the pan from the heat while you do it. Any kind of small thin fish or fish fillet can be used for this recipe.

Depending on the size of your pan, add half of the butter for two fish or a quarter if only one fish will fit.

1 Place the flour in a large flat-bottomed bowl or plate. Dip each fish in the flour, making sure it is well-coated on both sides.

2 Melt the butter in a non-stick pan over a low heat. Add a drop of oil to the pan to prevent the butter from burning.

Ingredients

4 skinned
sole fillets

125 g (4 oz)
butter

1 lemon

90 g (3 oz)
plain flour

30 g (1 oz)
finely chopped
parsley

salt

3 Add the fish to the pan and cook over a low heat. After about 5 minutes, flip the fish with a slotted spatula. Cook for another 5 minutes. Season with salt.

4 While the fish is cooking, squeeze the juice from the lemon.

5 When the fish is almost cooked, pour half the lemon juice over the fish and cook for 1 more minute. Slip the fish onto a serving dish and cook the rest.

Utensils

FRYING PAN

SLOTTED SPATULA

LEMON SQUEEZER

Clafoutis

Cherry tart

This tasty dessert is quick to make and to eat! It is a speciality of Limousin in central France. Its name comes from a **dialect** word *clafir*, which means 'to fill'. The original recipe uses whole cherries with their stones, but it is a good idea to remove the stones before you begin, or buy cherries with the stones already removed.

Ingredients

450 g
(1 lb)
ripe cherries

3 eggs

45 g (1½ oz)
icing sugar

200 ml
(7 fl oz)
milk

butter to
grease the
tart dish

TIPS & TRICKS

If cherries are not in season, replace them with the same quantity of any kind of berry or fruit used in cooking. Always use protective oven gloves when putting things into, or taking them out of, the oven.

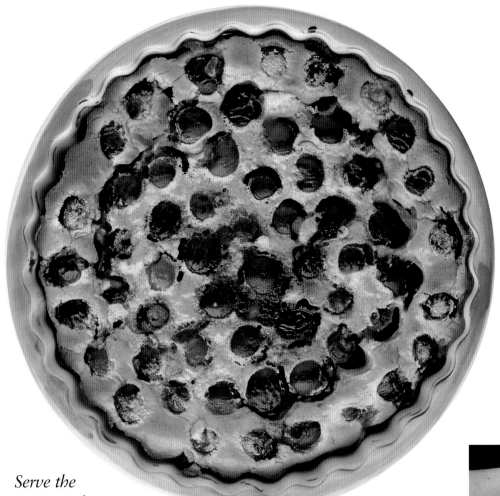

Serve the tart straight from the oven with vanilla ice cream, or let it cool and serve with whipped cream.

1 Wash the cherries under cold running water, drain well and pat dry with a clean cloth. Remove the stems and the stones.

Utensils

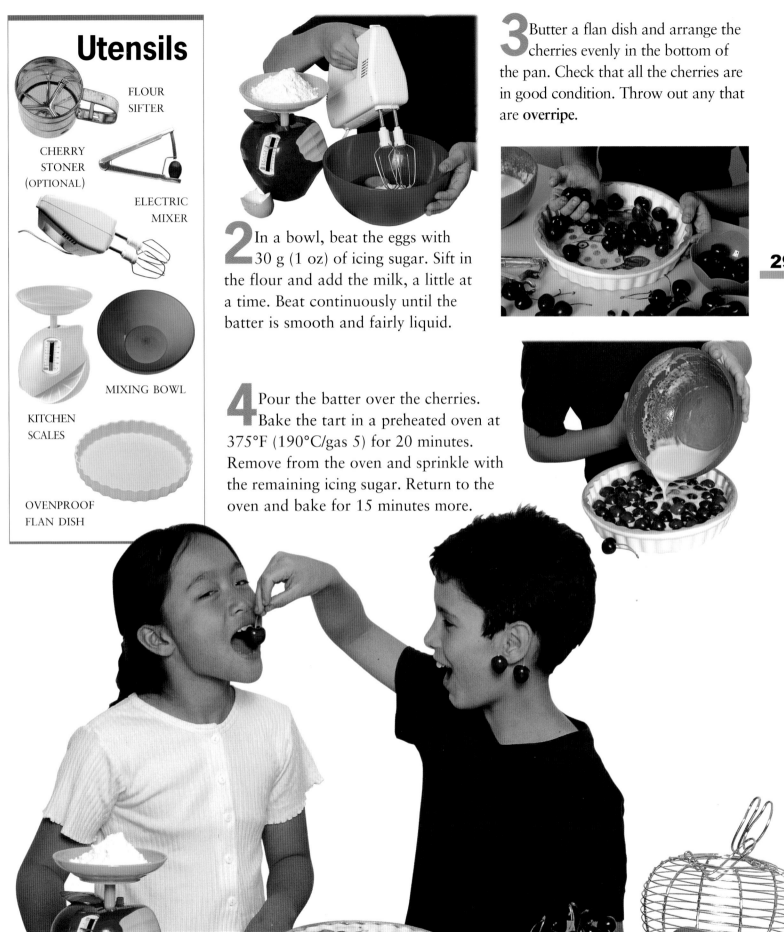

FLOUR SIFTER

CHERRY STONER (OPTIONAL)

ELECTRIC MIXER

MIXING BOWL

KITCHEN SCALES

OVENPROOF FLAN DISH

2 In a bowl, beat the eggs with 30 g (1 oz) of icing sugar. Sift in the flour and add the milk, a little at a time. Beat continuously until the batter is smooth and fairly liquid.

3 Butter a flan dish and arrange the cherries evenly in the bottom of the pan. Check that all the cherries are in good condition. Throw out any that are **overripe**.

4 Pour the batter over the cherries. Bake the tart in a preheated oven at 375°F (190°C/gas 5) for 20 minutes. Remove from the oven and sprinkle with the remaining icing sugar. Return to the oven and bake for 15 minutes more.

Tarte aux fraises

Strawberry tart

France is the third largest producer of strawberries in the world. It is not surprising, then, that the French were the inventors of this delicious tart. Strawberries are grown in the Rhone Valley, Brittany and other areas of France. They are full of vitamins and are very good for you.

Ingredients

250 g
(8 oz)
plain flour

125 g
(4 oz)
butter

2 egg yolks

75 g
(2½ oz) sugar

200 g (7 oz)
strawberry jam

1 kg (2.2 lb)
clean, fresh
strawberries

dried beans

1 Place the flour in a bowl. Add the butter and rub it in with your fingers until the mixture has the consistency of bread crumbs. Stir in the separated egg yolks, then bring the pastry together into a ball. Wrap it in plastic wrap and place in the fridge for about 30 minutes.

5 **Dilute** the jam with 2–3 tablespoons of warm water. Use a new, clean pastry brush to paint the top of the strawberries with the jam. Remove from the dish and serve at room temperature with ice cream or whipped cream.

Utensils

MIXING BOWL

BAKING SHEET

ROLLING PIN

PASTRY BRUSH

PIE DISH WITH LOOSE BOTTOM

2 Sprinke flour on a rolling pin and roll out the pastry on a floured work surface until it is about 5 mm (¼ in) thick.

4 Remove the pastry from the oven and throw out the paper and beans. Arrange the strawberries, pointed end facing upwards, on the pastry base.

3 Use the pastry to line a buttered and floured 26-cm (10-in) diameter loose-bottomed pie dish. Cover with a sheet of baking paper and fill with dried beans. Bake in a preheated oven at 350°F (180°C/gas 4) for about 20 minutes.

TIPS & TRICKS

Ask an adult to help you separate the egg yolks from the egg whites. If strawberries are out of season, replace them with the same quantity of raspberries.

Mousse au chocolat

Chocolate mousse

Soft, fluffy and sweet, mousse is almost pure chocolate and will be a favourite with your family and friends. Chocolate mousse is one of the easiest French desserts to make. It became a popular treat in the 1970s with the introduction of **nouvelle cuisine**. The best part about this recipe is clearing up and licking the spoons!

1 Put the chocolate in a small saucepan with the milk and then put the saucepan into a larger pan of cold water. Place over a medium heat, and stir until the chocolate melts.

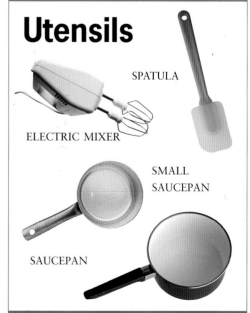

2 In a bowl, beat the **separated** egg yolks with the sugar until they are pale and creamy. Stir it into the melted chocolate.

Utensils

SPATULA

ELECTRIC MIXER

SMALL SAUCEPAN

SAUCEPAN

3 Beat the egg whites with a pinch of salt until they form stiff peaks. **Fold** the beaten egg whites into the chocolate, taking care that the egg whites do not lose their stiffness.

4 Beat the cream with an electric or hand-held whisk until thick. Fold it carefully into the chocolate and egg mixture.

Take care when melting the chocolate. Ask an adult to help you separate the egg yolks from the whites. Do not over-whip the cream in step 4, or it will turn into butter.

5 Transfer the mousse mixture into individual dessert dishes or one large serving bowl. Leave in the fridge for at least 4 hours before serving. Add whipped cream if desired.

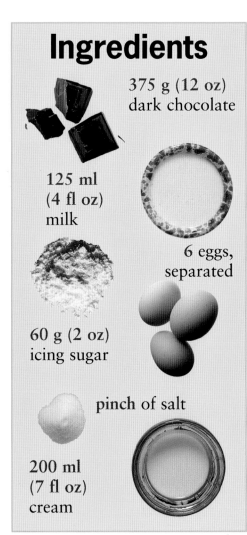

Ingredients

375 g (12 oz) dark chocolate

125 ml (4 fl oz) milk

6 eggs, separated

60 g (2 oz) icing sugar

pinch of salt

200 ml (7 fl oz) cream

Profiteroles

Profiteroles

You may have seen this rich-looking dessert in the window of bakeries many times. Now you can make it at home. To make things easier, you can buy the pastry cases ready-made. Then just fill them with ice cream, dip them in chocolate and decorate with whipped cream.

Ingredients

200 g (7 oz) dark chocolate

300 g (10 oz) ready-made choux pastry cases

300 g (10 oz) vanilla ice cream

250 ml (9 fl oz) whipping cream

1 Carefully use a knife to break up the chocolate. Tip it into a small saucepan and then put the pan into a larger pan of cold water. Place the saucepan over a medium heat and melt the chocolate.

TIPS & TRICKS

Take the ice cream out of the freezer just before you begin to fill the profiteroles. If you take it out too early it will melt while you work. You can also try filling the profiteroles with vanilla custard or whipped cream instead of the ice cream. You could add some fruit sauce on top of everything.

2 Make a small hole in each pastry case. Using a pastry chef's syringe, fill each one with ice cream.

3 Arrange the filled profiteroles one on top of the other in a pyramid shape. Use a little of the melted chocolate to stick them together.

Place attractive blobs or swirls of cream all over the profiterole pyramid.

4 Pour the remaining chocolate over the top so that it runs down the sides. Beat the cream until it is thick. Fill the syringe with the whipped cream and decorate the stack of profiteroles.

Utensils

ELECTRIC MIXER

KNIFE

PASTRY CHEF'S SYRINGE

SPATULA

Crème brûlée

Crème brûlée

Crème brûlée means 'burnt custard' in French, but this dessert is not actually burnt. When grilled, the brown sugar on the top forms a melt-in-the-mouth crust, which combines well with the creamy vanilla custard underneath. To really enjoy crème brûlée, serve it while it is still a little warm.

1 Ask an adult to separate the egg yolks from the whites. Then, in a bowl, beat the separated egg yolks with the sugar until they are pale and creamy.

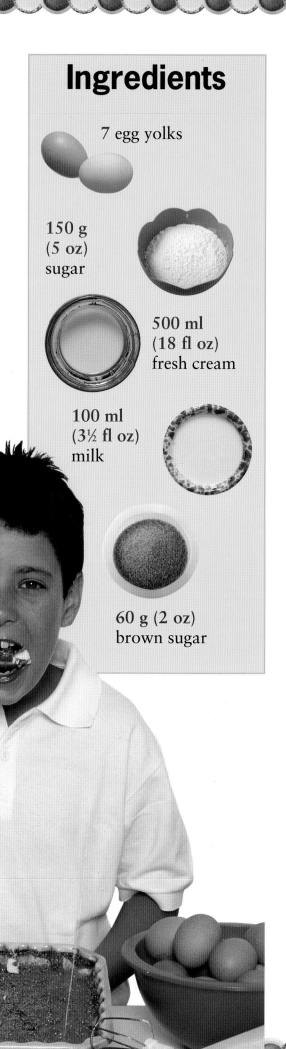

Ingredients

7 egg yolks

150 g (5 oz) sugar

500 ml (18 fl oz) fresh cream

100 ml (3½ fl oz) milk

60 g (2 oz) brown sugar

TIPS & TRICKS

Ask an adult to help you place the roasting pan in the oven. You must be careful not to spill water in the oven. When checking to see if it is cooked, and when grilling the sugar, remember to wear thick oven gloves.

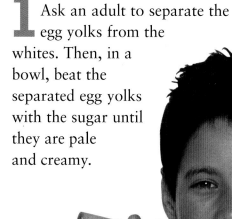

2 Heat the cream and milk together. Just before they boil, remove from the heat and pour them into the egg and sugar mixture, beating continuously.

To test whether the crème brûlée is cooked, insert a cake tester or toothpick into it. If the tester comes out dry and clean, it is ready.

Utensils

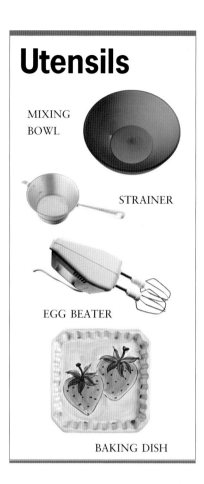

MIXING BOWL

STRAINER

EGG BEATER

BAKING DISH

3 Filter the mixture using a strainer.

4 Pour the mixture into a buttered ovenproof dish. Put the dish in a larger dish or pan, such as a roasting pan, filled with cold water. Place both dishes in a preheated oven at 350°F (180°C/gas 4), and cook for 1 hour. Ask an adult to help you with this.

5 Remove from the oven and set aside to cool. Sprinkle with the brown sugar and place under the grill for 5 minutes until the sugar is brown and crisp.

Glossary

butler the head male servant of a household, in charge of supervising other servants and serving meals.

chop to cut into tiny, fine pieces using a knife or food processor.

consistency the degree of firmness of a mixture of ingredients.

dialect a variation of a language in a particular region.

dilute to make a liquid thinner by adding water.

first course the first part of an elaborate dinner.

fold to blend an ingredient into a mixture by very gently turning one part over another.

French cuisine the French style or way of cooking food.

Gruyère cheese a pale yellow Swiss cheese.

ladleful adding the amount of liquid that fills a ladle, a utensil with a cup-shaped bowl.

marinade to soak food in a liquid mixture, usually of vinegar or wine, oil, herbs and spices, for a period of time before cooking.

nouvelle cuisine a style of cooking in the 1970s, using fresh ingredients, a variety of foods, and light sauces, served in a decorative way.

nutritious a food that is healthy to eat and provides a lot of nourishment.

overripe fruit or vegetables that are past their best appearance and texture.

pinch a small amount of an ingredient added to a mixture.

sautéed to cook or brown foods in a pan containing a small quantity of butter or oil.

savoury something that is pleasant in taste and not sweet.

separate to divide an egg's yolk from its white. Both can be used at different stages of a recipe.

sift to separate out any coarse grains of flour so only fine flour is used.

sprinkle to scatter in separate drops.

trim to remove the extra or unwanted parts of a food item.

wedges thick slices.

Index